P9-DEZ-160

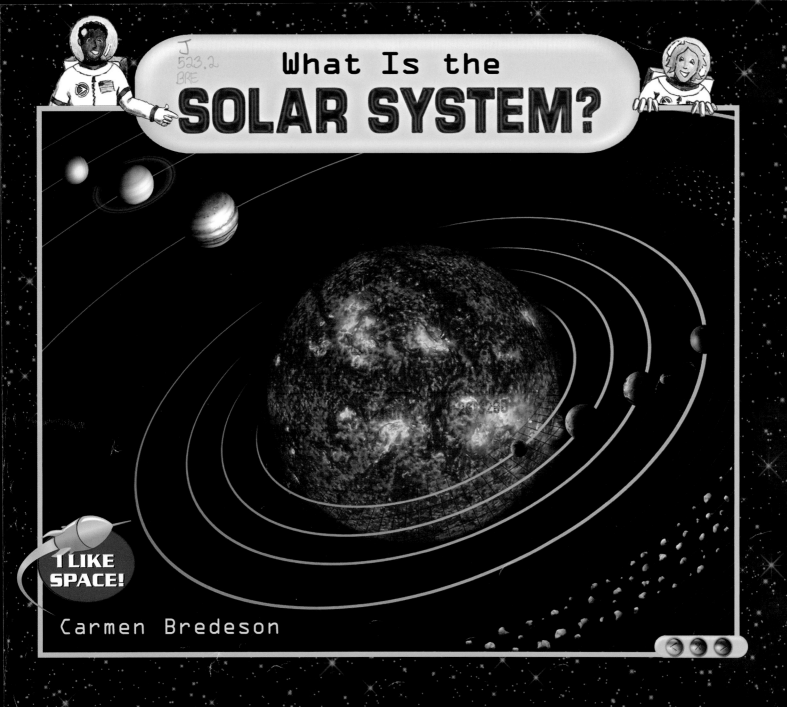

What Is the
SOLAR SYSTEM?

I LIKE SPACE!

Carmen Bredeson

asteroid (AS tur oyd)
A rock in space.

atmosphere (AT muhs feer)
The air around Earth.

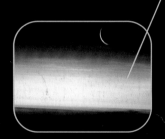

dwarf (dworf)
Small for its kind.

gravity (GRA vih tee)
The force that pulls one thing toward another. When you jump up, Earth's gravity pulls you back down.

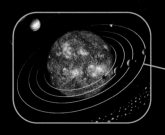

orbit (OR bit)
To go around something in space.

CONTENTS

What is the solar system?

Sol is another word for Sun.

The solar system is the Sun's family.

Planets, moons, asteroids, and comets are part of the family.

They all go around, or orbit, the Sun.

comet

Fun Fact

The Sun is not the only star to have a family of planets. Scientists have found more than two hundred planets orbiting other stars.

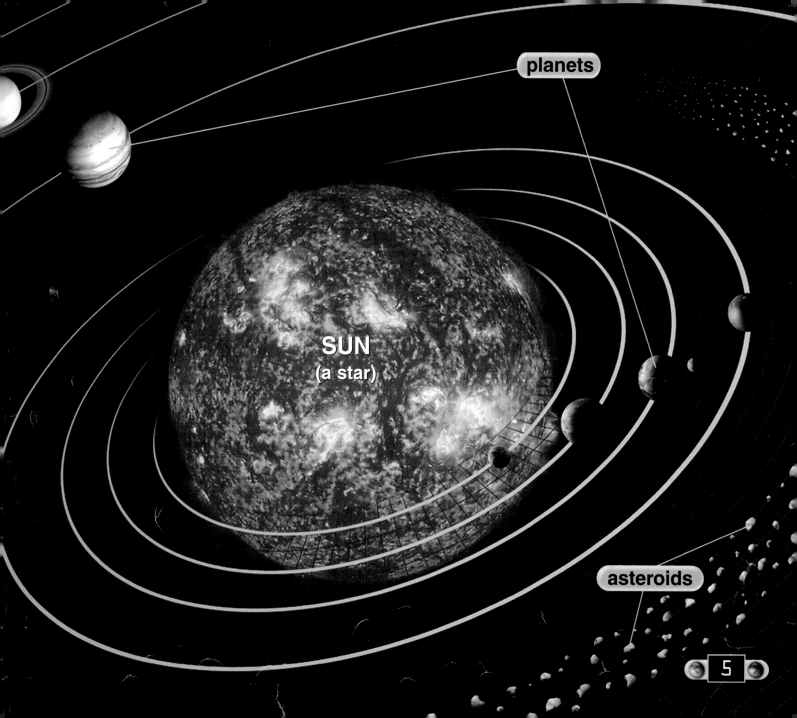

planets

SUN
(a star)

asteroids

What is a planet?

A planet is a big round object
that orbits a star. Earth is a planet.
It orbits the Sun.

The Moon is also big and round.
But the Moon is not a planet.
It does not orbit the Sun.
The Moon orbits Earth.

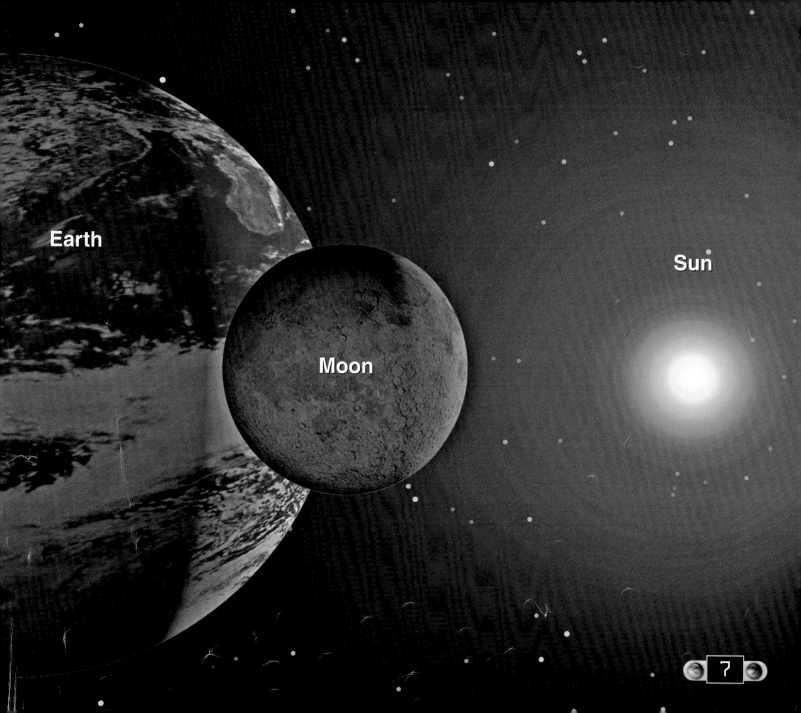

Earth

Moon

Sun

How many planets are there?

Sun

Jupiter

Earth

Mercury

Mars

Venus

Fun Fact

A spaceship to Pluto blasted off in January 2006. It should get to Pluto around 2015.

Saturn

Uranus

Neptune

Pluto
(dwarf planet)

There are eight planets in the solar system. In August 2006, scientists said that Pluto was no longer a planet. Pluto is now called a **dwarf planet**. Pluto is smaller than the Moon.

What are planets made of?

Mercury, Venus, Earth, and Mars are made of rock.

Jupiter, Saturn, Uranus, and Neptune are made of gas.

You could not stand on a gas planet.

It would be like trying to stand on a cloud.

This close-up photo of Jupiter shows swirls of clouds and a giant storm called the Great Red Spot. The Great Red Spot is as large as three Earths!

Which planet is the biggest? Which one is the smallest?

Jupiter is *HUGE!*
It is the biggest planet in
the solar system.
More than 1,000 Earths
could fit inside Jupiter.
Mercury is the smallest planet.
It is very, very hot since it
is so close to the Sun.

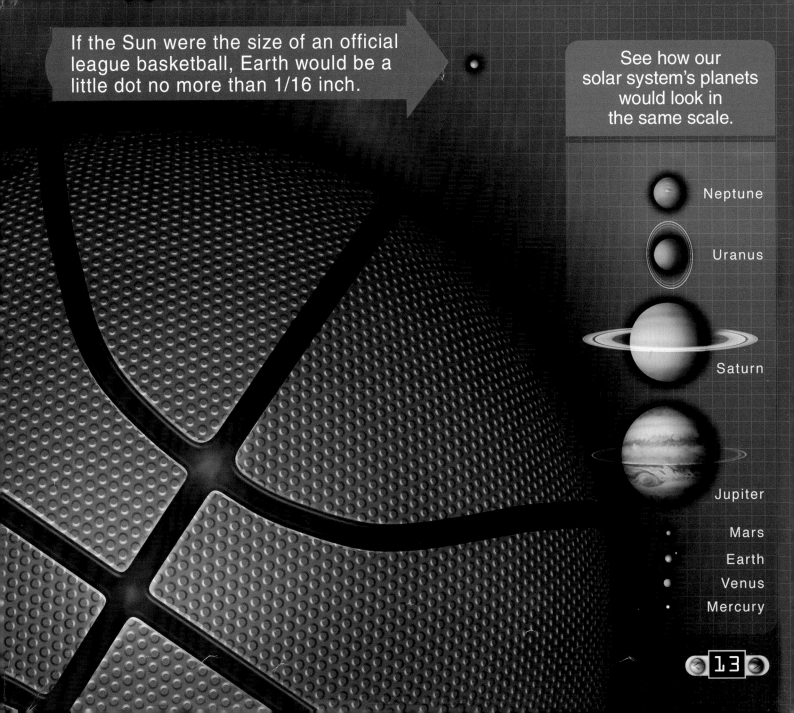

If the Sun were the size of an official league basketball, Earth would be a little dot no more than 1/16 inch.

See how our solar system's planets would look in the same scale.

Neptune

Uranus

Saturn

Jupiter

Mars

Earth

Venus

Mercury

Jupiter's four biggest moons: Io, Europa, Ganymede, and Callisto

Venus and Mercury have no moons.

Earth has one Moon.

Jupiter has about 60 moons!

One of Jupiter's moons, Ganymede, is the biggest moon in the solar system.

Ganymede is about the size of Mars.

Fun Fact

Scientists believe our Moon used to be part of Earth.

Earth

Earth's Moon

What are Saturn's rings made of?

Saturn's sparkling rings are made mostly of ice.

Some of the chunks are bigger than a house.

Some are as small as a piece of dust.

Sun shining through the rings lights them up.

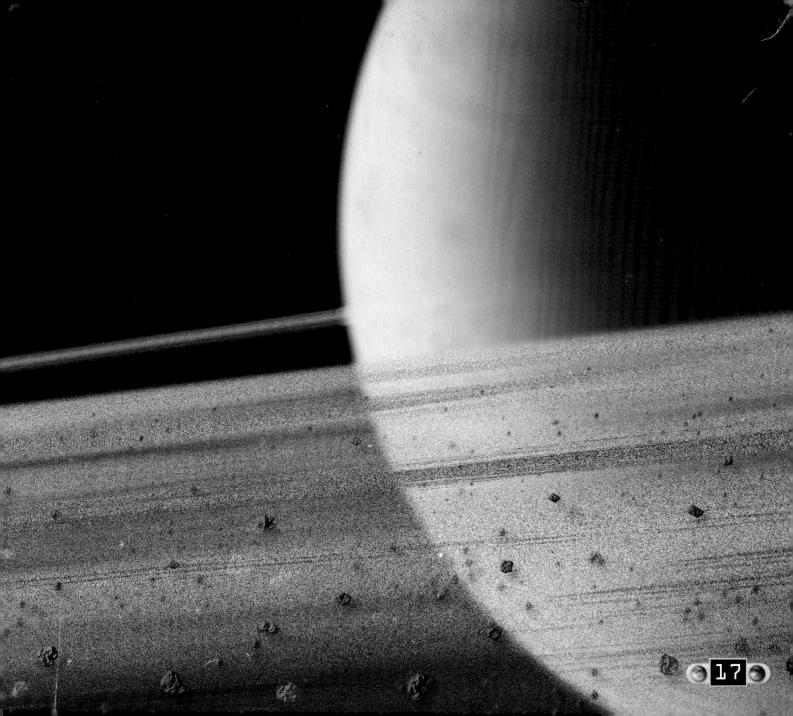

What are asteroids?

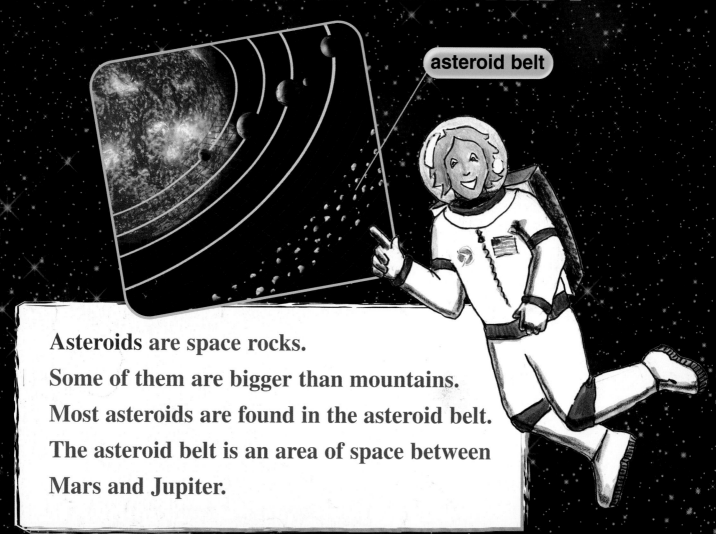

asteroid belt

Asteroids are space rocks.

Some of them are bigger than mountains.

Most asteroids are found in the asteroid belt.

The asteroid belt is an area of space between Mars and Jupiter.

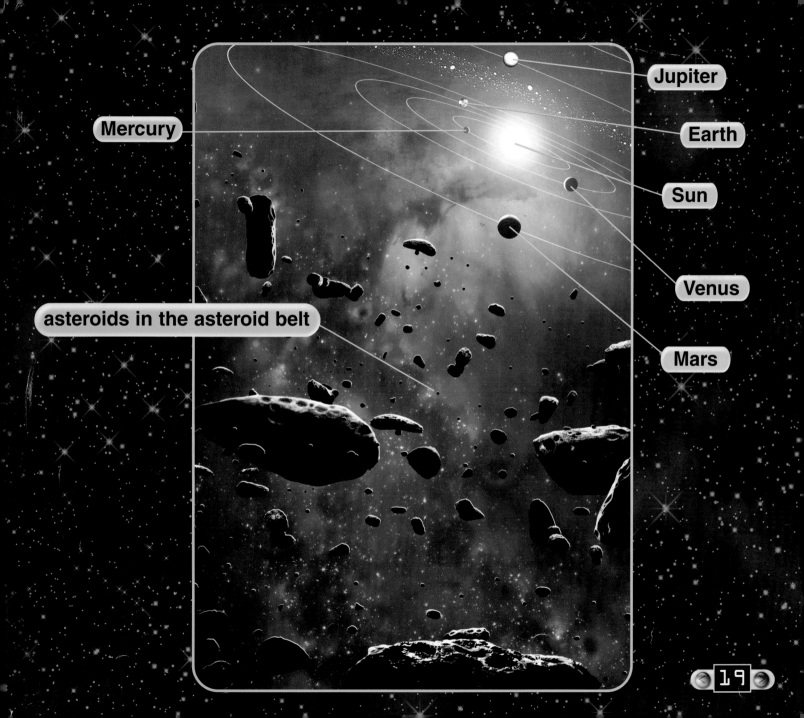

Jupiter

Mercury

Earth

Sun

Venus

asteroids in the asteroid belt

Mars

What are comets?

Comets are big loose balls of dust and ice.
They orbit the Sun far out in space.
When a comet travels close
to the Sun, it heats up.
Some of the ice turns into gas
and makes a long, glowing tail.

Fun Fact

Some comets orbit the Sun about every three years. Other comets may take thousands of years to go once around the Sun.

What are meteorites?

This meteorite was found in Arizona.

Some comets and asteroids lose pieces of rock and dust. The pieces zoom through space. A few of them reach Earth's atmosphere. Most of them burn up. The ones that land on Earth are called meteorites.

This is a drawing of
a rock burning in
Earth's atmosphere.

Fun Fact

Space rocks that burn up in
Earth's atmosphere are called
meteors or shooting stars.

What is far out in the solar system?

An area of space past Neptune is called the Kuiper (KY pur) Belt.

Scientists use strong telescopes to find objects in this area.

At least one object is a dwarf planet larger than Pluto.

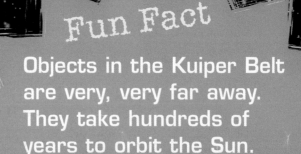

Fun Fact

Objects in the Kuiper Belt are very, very far away. They take hundreds of years to orbit the Sun.

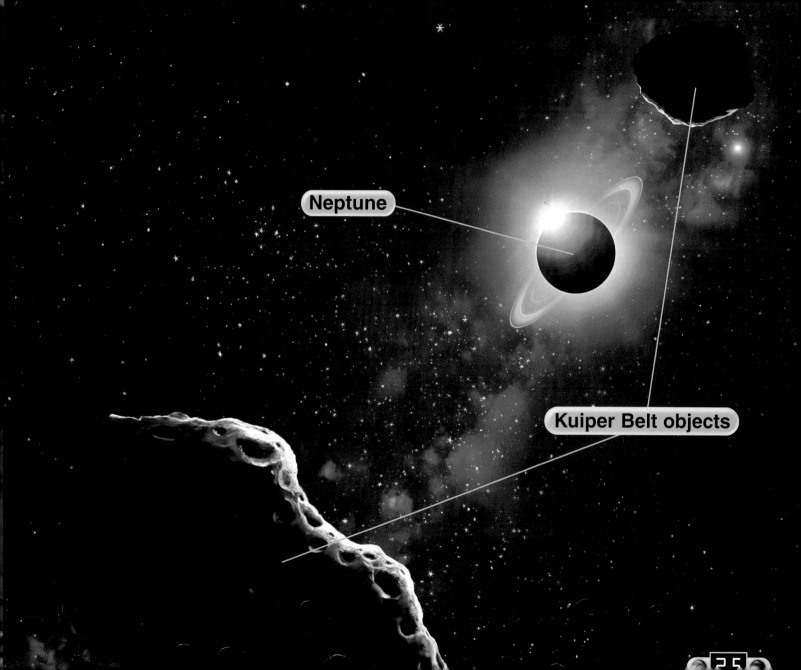

Neptune

Kuiper Belt objects

Where does our solar system end?

The Oort Cloud is way, way out at the edge of the solar system. Some comets are found in this area of space. Anything farther away than the Oort Cloud would not be part of our solar system.

Sun, planets, and Kuiper Belt

Oort Cloud

What is special about Earth's place in the solar system?

If Earth were farther away from the Sun, its water would freeze. If Earth were closer to the Sun, its oceans would boil away. Earth is in just the right place for water to exist. Plants, animals, and people all need water to live and grow.

Astronomers (uh STRAH nuh murz)
use telescopes to study space.

Mission controllers
guide spaceships to the planets
or into Earth orbit.

Geologists (jee AH loh jists)
study what the planets are made of.

Science teachers
help students learn about space.

LEARN MORE

Books

Kortenkamp, Steve. *Why Isn't Pluto a Planet?: A Book About Planets.* Mankato, Minn.: Capstone Press, 2007.

Nicolson, Cynthia Pratt. *Discover the Planets.* Toronto: Kids Can Press, 2005.

Rau, Dana Meachen. *Spinning in Space: A Book About the Planets.* Minneapolis, Minn.: Picture Window Books, 2006.

Web Sites

Arnett, Bill. The Nine (Eight) Planets for Kids.
http://nineplanets.org/

NASA/GSFC. Star Child.
http://starchild.gsfc.nasa.gov/docs/StarChild/StarChild.html

INDEX

To Kate, our shining star

Enslow Elementary, an imprint of Enslow Publishers, Inc.

Enslow Elementary® is a registered trademark of Enslow Publishers, Inc.

Library of Congress Cataloging-in-Publication Data

Bredeson, Carmen.
   What is the solar system? / Carmen Bredeson.
      p. cm. — (I like space!)
      Summary: "An introduction to our solar system for new readers"—Provided
by publisher.
   Includes bibliographical references and index.
   ISBN-13: 978-0-7660-2944-6 (alk. paper)
   ISBN-10: 0-7660-2944-1 (alk. paper)
   1. Solar system—Juvenile literature. 2. Planets—Juvenile literature. I. Title.
   QB501.3.B744 2008
   523.2-dc22   2007025552

Printed in the United States of America

10 9 8 7 6 5 4 3 2

To Our Readers: We have done our best to make sure all Internet Addresses in this book were
active and appropriate when we went to press. However, the author and the publisher have
no control over and assume no liability for the material available on those Internet sites or on
other Web sites they may link to. Any comments or suggestions can be sent by e-mail to
comments@enslow.com or to the address on the back cover.

Cover Photograph: David A. Hardy/Photo Researchers, Inc.

Illustration Credits: Carl M. Feryok (astronauts)

Photo Credits: Atlas Photo Bank/Photo Researchers, Inc., p. 23; David A. Hardy/Photo
Researchers, Inc., p. 27 (inset); Courtesy NASA/JPL-Caltech, pp. 1, 2 (orbit), 4–5, 11, 14, 15,
18; H. Mikuz, Crni Vrh Observatory, Slovenia, p. 21; Jon Lomberg/Photo Researchers, Inc.,
p. 27; Mark Garlick/Photo Researchers, Inc., pp. 2 (asteroid), 19, 25; NASA, p. 10; NASA and
European Space Agency, p. 13; NASA-GRC, p. 16; NASA-MSFC, pp. 2 (atmosphere), 17;
Shutterstock, blue starfield background and pp. 8–9, 22, 29; Steve A. Munsinger/Photo
Researchers, Inc., pp. 6–7.

Series Literacy Consultant:
Allan A. De Fina, Ph.D.
Past President of the New Jersey Reading Association
Chairperson, Department of Literacy Education
New Jersey City University, Jersey City, New Jersey

Series Science Consultant:
Marianne J. Dyson
Former NASA Flight Controller
Science Writer
www.mdyson.com

Enslow Elementary
an imprint of
Enslow Publishers, Inc.
40 Industrial Road
Box 398
Berkeley Heights, NJ 07922
USA
http://www.enslow.com